Fight for Your Story

Fight for Your Story

Copyright © 2018 by Kay Cervetti

ISBN 978-0-9701781-1-4

All rights reserved. No part of this book may be reproduced or transmitted in any form or by any means, electronic or mechanical, including photocopying, recording or by any information storage and retrieval system, without permission in writing from the copyright owner. For information on distribution rights, royalties, derivative works or licensing opportunities on behalf of this content or work, please contact the publisher at the address below.

Printed in the United States of America.

Although the author and publisher have made every effort to ensure that the information in this book was correct and accurate at press time, the author and publisher do not assume and hereby disclaim any liability to any party for any loss, damage, or disruption caused from acting upon the information in this book or by errors or omissions, whether such errors or omissions result from negligence, accident, or any other cause.

Scripture quotations taken from the New American Standard Bible® (NASB),
Copyright © 1960, 1962, 1963, 1968, 1971, 1972, 1973, 1975, 1977, 1995 by The Lockman Foundation.
Used by permission. www.Lockman.org.

Camel Knee Publishing
2816 Scenic Drive
Cedar Falls, IA. 50613
www.kaycervetti.org

Fight for Your Story

Live the story you want to tell

Kay Cervetti

Fight for Your Story

Acknowledgments

I could not have published this book without the continuous support from my children. I treasure every moment where we have chosen to laugh in the face of adversity because it has made us the strong, resilient family we are today. Thank you Ashley, Blake, and Brady for your love, grace, encouragement, and inspiration. You mean so much to me. I love you.

Fight for Your Story

TABLE OF CONTENTS

Introduction	9
Chapter 1: Who Am I?	11
Chapter 2: What Love Feels Like	21
Chapter 3: No Matter What	37
Chapter 4: Necessary Endings	45
Chapter 5: Necessary Beginnings	53
Chapter 6: Necessary Pain	61
Chapter 7: Good, Better, Best	75
Excerpt from the workbook	83
To Whom it May Concern	101
About the Author	103

Fight for Your Story

Introduction

Sometimes life takes us places we never expected to go. And in those places God writes a story we never thought would be ours. This book is the simple truth about who I was and who I am. The details are raw, honest and beautiful. It has taken me 59 years to accept the reality of my childhood. I couldn't bring myself to accept that my brokenness wasn't entirely my fault. I owned every mistake that I made. I just didn't completely understand it. When the pieces started to fall into place, I finally knew the truth and it literally changed my life. There was amazing freedom that came, and continues to come. In hindsight, my life finally made sense. I began to see what I had not been able to see. In a sense, the scales fell from my eyes.

This book may be hard for some people to read, for various reasons. Some people begin to wiggle in their seat because it makes them feel uncomfortable. It may hit pretty close to home. Some people just cannot wrap their mind around what actually happened, or didn't happen. Sometimes knowing truth can be really hard.

If we dare to look, we often catch glimpses of God at work in our lives. When the Spirit of God shows up, something sacred happens. The presence of God heals the broken places. That is when we find and become our true selves. Becoming who God designed us to be is not easy, but it is in the fight for your story, that your story becomes your story. It is always worth it.

Proverbs 4:7
The beginning of wisdom is this:
Acquire wisdom;
And with all your acquiring,
get understanding.

Who Am I?

This never would have been the story I would have chosen for myself. Never. And I do mean never. Getting to this point in life was a lot of work.

For the record, first and foremost, I'm a mom. I'm also a health educator, teacher, and fitness professional who believes everyone should live the story they want to tell. Every. Single. Day. It's never too late to follow your dreams.

Off the record, I love to laugh. You could describe me as an extroverted introvert who loves a new challenge. I am not a runner at heart, but I run. I love chai tea and the Hallmark Channel. I was adopted along with my twin sister by parents who weren't equipped to be parents.

At 37 years of age I found my biological family, and my life hasn't been the same since.

You see, once upon a time I was a little girl that had big dreams. I dreamt of happy days when balloons went up and confetti came down. That was the way life should be. I loved to laugh and often spent my days dreaming because my home life had left me with deep wounds and absolutely no skills for the future.

I was sexually molested by an uncle and raped as a teenager, but I clung to the dreams deep within my heart. My mother refused to believe the accusations about my uncle, even though they also had happened to other family members. The circle of people I could depend on to keep me safe became very small, but my dream lived on. The constant fighting and swearing and hitting at home had taken its toll.

By the age of 16 I had survived the suicide temptations, only to find myself pregnant by the first man who told me that he loved me. Having been adopted, I decided to give the baby up for adoption but my parents would not hear it, and made the arrangements for me to have an abortion. At the age of 18, I married the only man who told me that he loved me, in an attempt to right all of the wrongs. Just a few months into the marriage I found out I did not have the tools to fix all that was broken. In shame, I divorced him a year later and told myself that I would never make that mistake again.

Relying on the advice of my parents, I dated and married a man who was perfect in their eyes, and the furthest thing from my Prince Charming. Just two short years later I found myself divorced again, and now a single mother to a toddler. My dream was now buried deep in my heart, and the days for dreaming were few and far between. In my early 20s, working a good job, and showing promising parenting skills, life began to look up. Marriage number three was short lived also and revelation finally came when I realized I was the common denominator in all of those marriages. Marriage number four lasted 18 years. In those 18 years I grew, I learned, I gave thanks. I became a different woman.

I was a follower. I was never a leader. I made a fine mess of my early years. Seems like another lifetime really. I have quite a past. Failed relationships, rejection, love, lies, and more. Colorful. Shameful. Educational.

By all rights, I shouldn't be as happy as I am. I had been rejected the day I was born and subjected to a home life of silence. I was never given permission to have emotions. Nothing was modeled for me. I didn't know how to react, how to feel. I was taught to be a keeper of secrets.

All of my life I thought I was broken and needed fixing, but the truth was I was hurt and needed healing. Those are two very different concepts. Being broken meant there was something intrinsically wrong with me that needed fixing. And, if I wasn't fixed, I'd never be right. That's a scary concept for a child. Being hurt and in need of healing was a much more manageable concept. Doctors are in the business of healing people all the time. That doesn't seem near as daunting.

I learned about my adoption at the age of five on the Whittier Elementary School playground. When that revelation spilled out one day at recess, I was shocked at what I heard and couldn't even begin to comprehend the meaning of adoption. It had been meant to remain a secret, and although coveted by my classmates, I didn't like anything about it.

Just that quickly adoption had become part of my identity. As I grew up adoption was just one of many identities I would embrace through the years. Adoption to a child can be scary and lonely. There were no guarantees that my new family would be my forever family. What followed became an identity crisis of sorts. For too many years I let my failures define me, my friends and family define me, my own flailing self worth define me. What I believed about myself affected who I spent time with and how big my dreams were, or weren't.

For a lot of adoptees, we have no idea who we really are. It's like being in the witness protection program from birth. Our pasts have been wiped out and we began living life according to other people's expectations. We don't know any better, until we grow up.

I always believed that my adoption experience was amazing because everyone around me kept telling me that I should be grateful to these parents who made so many sacrifices for me. When in reality, it was a far cry from the picture that was always painted for me.

Along with the adoption label, I was always known as 'one of the twins'. And, being a twin was a pretty big thing. It landed us in a photo shoot for our local newspaper when we were just 3 years old. The biggest blessing in the world is to have someone your own age with whom you can laugh, play, fight, and cry.

At the age of eight I began a 10-year competitive swimming career. I swam twelve months out of the year. Swimming became my home away from home. I found approval and acceptance in the water. I worked hard in the water and had hundreds of ribbons, medals, and records to prove it. During those years I became known as a really good swimmer. Another label, a good label.

I was an above average student, and in middle school I discovered my passion for the English language. The written language, and the spoken language. I loved to do research and write papers. I was pretty creative. Although I was always known as the quiet one, there was no shortage of thoughts going on under the surface.

Once I became old enough, I became involved in school music and sports. I was in track, swimming, gymnastics, softball, and cheerleading. I sang in the choir, and played the violin and string bass. In all honesty I was happiest when I was away from home, so activities were a welcome diversion.

I began teaching fitness classes in my mid 20's, and although I was always fairly athletic, standing in front of an aerobic class was quite another thing. I was working through my shyness. At times it was terrifying. I taught at several local organizations and then ventured out on my own. I began a non-profit organization (The Training Center) and offered fitness classes for $1/class. With a degree in Health Education, I incorporated healthy eating and weight loss classes. Over the years we lost hundreds of pounds together, and people got healthier. We promote fitness, faith, and family.

I became a mom for the first time to a beautiful baby girl named Ashley at the age of 22 (marriage number two). My boys were born 10 and 12 years later (marriage number four). It would be totally fair to say that I didn't have it all figured out yet, but there was a never ending love for this bundle of blonde hair and giggles. Ashley is one of the funniest people I know. Although we had some rough patches in high school and beyond, I am very proud of her. Ashley was my constant as we bounced from relationship to relationship. Although I was doing the best that I could, it wasn't fair to her. She didn't get started on a good foundation, but she learned and grew and became the woman she is today. Ashley and Travis made me a grandma to five beautiful and spirited gals. I get to do life with them day in and day out.

    I homeschooled my boys on and off in elementary school when one was being bullied, and the other wasn't putting in enough effort. Those are some of the very best memories of our lives.

    Blake was extremely disciplined, and exceptionally bright, and all I had to do was have his lesson plan on the counter for him. He worked down the list crossing things off, and smiled at his accomplishments. He has an incredible work ethic. On the other hand, Brady always said, "This would be a great day for a field trip." Every. Single. Day. Brady stretched me in every way. In the 5th grade he decided he was going to repeat 5th grade, and I said "Not on my shift." I pulled him out of school and homeschooled just him. I was taking college classes at the time, so when I packed my bag for the day, I packed his bag and off to college we went together. On the campus, my friend, mentor, and professor Oakland became his Principal Oakland and we kept his feet to the fire academically. I could not have done it without the help of so many great friends. The next year he moved to the 6th grade with the rest of his class, and he says to this day that those were some of his favorite memories.

Mayo Clinic says I'm at the fitness level of a 25 year old male. While that was never part of the plan, it's created the opportunity for me to do some outrageous activities, and meet the most interesting people.

I became a runner in 2013 when I told my boys, Blake and Brady, to not buy me anything for Mother's Day, but instead let's plan an adventure that we could all do together. I thought we would go somewhere for a weekend, hang out, go out to eat, and make memories. To my surprise they signed me up for a half marathon. I was a non-runner before that, not running more than three miles, and I might add it was not fast. Crossing the finish line was the miracle.

I spent the summer of 2013 running on trails, roads, and treadmills. It was the hottest summer on record. Of course it was. That September I ran my first half marathon with my college age boys. There were so many memories we shared in 13.1 miles, but my favorite became the Mile 8 photo, which would become a tradition at every long run to follow. In the fall of 2017 we completed the Chicago Half Marathon together. It was my 20th half marathon.

In the fall of 2015, I signed up to run the I-35 challenge. It is an event where you run a half marathon or marathon in Kansas City on Saturday, and then drive up Interstate 35 and run either a half marathon or marathon in Des Moines the next day. I ran a full marathon in both cities. It was an amazing accomplishment and my boys were at the finish line. My boys have changed my life in ways I never could have imagined.

I graduated from The University of Northern Iowa at the age of 57 after 26 years. A dream realized. A huge dream realized. I started a masters program at the age of 58.

I'm a dreamer and I'm a lifelong learner. I'm a giver of grace and love. I still love to laugh. There is a lot of my story that still needs to be written.

What Love Feels Like

Love is growing up with a twin sister Sue, and a wiener dog named Tina. People try to compare it to having a sibling, but it's not the same as being a twin. We were always there for each other, even though our life experiences were very different.

There were so many times when having each other was all we had. I remember going to Disneyland in California in the late 1960's with my aunt and uncle (yes, THAT uncle). We rode the cable cars across the park. We thought it would take us back, but that return trip cost more money and my aunt and uncle were waiting for us back where we started. All out of options, we grabbed hands and followed the cables back to the other side of the park. We were terrified that we would never make it back to where we started. You never know how strong you are until you need to be strong. Being strong became second nature for me, for us.

We shared in countless experiences growing up together. We walked a mile to and from school in kindergarten every day. There is a lot of fun that can be had in 10 city blocks. We were inseparable really. We were in the same classroom until 3rd grade when someone decided that twins needed to be split up. I still remember that year.

Two heads were always better than one. We took turns peeking down the stairs while the other held our ankles. We snuck out on the roof of our 2-story home. Where one was, the other was close by. We always played together, and even carried snakes around in our pockets. We found creative and memorable ways to retrieve the ball from the neighbors yard. And most importantly, she kept my secrets and I kept hers, because that's what sisters do. Pinky promise forever.

My adoptive mom was diagnosed with breast cancer while I was in middle school. I remember being terrified that she was going to die. Cancer research wasn't as advanced as it is today and there were limited treatment options. They immediately scheduled a radical mastectomy. I remember my dad sitting down with my sister and I, and telling us that there would be big changes at home. He didn't elaborate, and I wondered what that meant. I understood that she was having major surgery but I didn't understand how that would change things at home. What I remember most was feeling sorry for her. As a teenager girl, I couldn't think of anything that would be worse. My heart was troubled, and I wondered in the back of my mind if my forever home would be forever. I wondered what would happen to us if she died. It was one of those things we never spoke about it.

    Another topic not open for discussion was my friendship with John. I remember him as the strong, silent type, and one of my very best friends in middle school. He was handsome and kind. We walked the halls together and posed for group pictures on the school steps. We were athletes. We went to the 9th grade dance together. After dancing a few times that night we ended the evening by going bowling. We exchanged letters over the summer when he was out of state, and our friendship grew. Without even knowing it, I gave him a piece of my heart that I could never get back. One autumn day, after walking me home from school several times, my mom saw us walking down the street. She was horrified. I couldn't grasp her concern, but she told my dad as soon as he got home from work. Over dinner that night my parents told me that John could not walk me home anymore. I was confused because he was the nicest guy I knew, and I was sure they would agree if they just knew him. There was no point in arguing my cause when I realized it was because John's dad was black, and his mom was white. They didn't approve. It was the 1970's after all. That was a conundrum to me, but their minds were made up. They were racist. And that's all there was to that. I remember the heartache that came with saying goodbye. He never reallly knew why we parted ways.

Between our junior and senior years of high school, Sue went to Australia through a foreign exchange program. And while I marveled at this opportunity for her, I didn't realize how abandoned I would feel. Of course I didn't. Going from being a team of two to an only child for eleven months was pretty lonely. And the parent/child gap at home widened. I became a voracious letter writer. We melted the miles between us with every letter. I still remember the day she came home. While we were celebrating at the airport, the dog managed to get on top of the table and eat the 'Welcome Home' cake. But I didn't care. She was finally home.

That fall, after graduation, Sue went off to college and I went to work. After college she moved a couple hours away, and I stayed close to our parents. I helped my parents run their errands, took their phone calls at all hours, and basically became the one responsible for helping out. Someone has to do it, and let's face it, it's usually the oldest or the closest. I happened to be both.

I have been in and out of love, to varying degrees, many times in my life. Love changes people in interesting ways. Love can cause us to live larger, to risk more. You don't even really have to understand it in order to experience it. Love always takes you on a journey.

I met a guy and fell in love for the first time at the age of 15. He was a hockey player with a great sense of humor, and a red Volkswagen. He also broke my heart. I remember that day. I was pretty sure the sun would never shine again, and even if it did, I doubted that I would notice. A first love is a forever love in some ways.

On my second marriage, and at the age of 22, I had my daughter. I was still pretty broken emotionally, but it was all I knew. My entire life had been one struggle after another. I was doing the best with what I had been given. One thing I knew for certain, I was hopelessly in love with this little girl. For the first time in my life I felt like I had purpose and direction.

I became a Christian when I was 25 years old. I fell madly in love with the Jesus of the Bible. I crawled to the foot of the cross every day, and breathed in His Word. For God's Words are life to those who find them, and health to their whole body. I memorized Scripture and camped on the promises of God. They were my lifeline and a never ending source of hope and love.

Up until this point love had always come at a price. The love I grew up with was manipulative, controlling, and broken. It was all I knew. I had glimpses of the real deal through the years but my brokenness prevented me from ever being able to commit to it. Those guys were boring and predictable. I wanted it all: passion, laughs and lots of adventure. God sent a true gentlemen my way but I was not in the place where I could see a future with him. He was grounded, honest, and pure in heart. I had none of those qualities, even though I desired them desperately. He had grown up with love in his home. He was so kind, generous, and faithful. I could see that it was very different from my experiences. His family was loving, caring and welcoming.

Now, nearly thirty years later, I still remember packing up and moving two hours from home to be with him. I left behind 11 years of employment with one company. We were engaged and I had a wedding dress. Our love was the real deal. My heart was so full of love for him. You don't get many moments like that in life. I certainly didn't. Somehow he saw the good in me that I couldn't see. If only I could have known then what I know now. Through the years the manipulation had eroded my confidence in my own ability to make decisions regarding my thoughts and feelings in a profound and lasting way. My mother told me if I married him she would never speak to me again. I rationalized my mother's behavior for many different reasons through the years. So, once again I trusted in someone who should have had my best interest at heart. The wedding dress went back but the memories we shared together could not be taken away. I will always remember that last New Years Eve we spent together. Walking away was the hardest thing I had ever done. To this day I don't know why I didn't have the courage to trust him with my future, but instead chose to fall back into the familiar, but broken. Even in my late 20's I was very much a reflection of my childhood environment. I just didn't know it yet.

    A few weeks later, and laid off from my job, I realized I was pregnant with our child, and now alone. I didn't know what to do. So I did what we as humans do so well. I repeated history with another abortion. Life had just gone from bad to worse. I can't even adequately describe the desperation. I know that is not what he would have chosen. He would have raised our child on his own. I took away his vote. I didn't tell him, before or after. But someone did. When he called me out of the blue, it caught me off guard. He wanted to know why I didn't let him raise our child. I had no words. It took me many years to come to terms with it, offer an apology for the hurt I caused, and the wounds I left behind, but most of all to ask for his forgiveness.

A few years later I married a man my mother approved of. I had my boys when I was 32 and 34, and God was teaching me about love through my children. Although far from perfect, I was experiencing change from the inside out.

I laid my hands on my kids and prayed God's Word over them. I prayed prayers of blessings over them before we went out the door to school. I silently prayed in the car, sitting in traffic, at the school, in church, at soccer games, and even at the police station. . . at all times and in all situations. Sometimes they were prayers of desperation, and sometimes they were prayers of protection and petition. Several times they were the prayers of a hopeless mother who knew not what to do, but knew that God knew what to do.

My oldest son nearly died from a tree nut allergy, and I didn't trust anyone with him more than I trusted Jesus. I read that verse that says, "Test me and see that I am not God," so I did. And, that wasn't the last time. I prayed prayers of healing, taking authority over sickness and disease. His health dramatically improved, and my faith grew.

As my children grew up, I grew up too. My childhood had left me with a deficit socially and emotionally. I had issues like insecurity, codependency, anger, guilt, shame, and condemnation. It's funny how life will bring you nose to nose with the opportunity to get healthy, spiritually and emotionally. And, it did. I was so desperate. I welcomed it. I went through every door God opened, running towards a dream of a happier life.

I did things that stretched my faith like teaching church through jail ministry and praying out loud for people. One day one of the sheriffs called me as they were releasing a gal I had met at the jail, and asked if I would take her to where she needed to go. I didn't even know where to go when she was released. I was learning how the system worked. What an education. When I arrived she was standing there with all of her belongings in a black garbage bag. As I was driving her home, I drove by our house and told her if she ever needed a place to go, she could always come stay at our house. Even at the time I thought to myself, "Do you even know what you are getting into?" Although I didn't know her that well, we had communicated by writing letters while she was incarcerated. Not long after that she moved in with us. She fit in with our six kids, and I'm not going to say it was perfect, but it was better than where she had been. We spent a lot of time together exercising, running errands, buying groceries, and planning her future. Soon after that she got a job and I provided transportation for awhile. Eventually she made a fresh start, moved out on her own, married a wonderful man and now has a family of her own. God amazes me.

    An empty nest taught me more about love, about how much I had changed through the years, and that I still hated being alone. I was not prepared for being alone. I wanted to hold onto my kids, to make life easy for them here so they would never leave. When I say I wanted to hold onto my kids, I mean I really wanted to hold onto them. I had worked myself out of my dream job and I hated it. But I had promised myself that their lives and experiences would be full. I had promised I would never sell them out for my personal gain or selfishness.

In hindsight I'm glad they chose colleges out of state. It was good for them and it was good for me. Somehow I hadn't been prepared for the empty nest and all that came with it. I really missed having my kids under my roof. They were so much fun. I liked myself best when I was with them. I could see myself in them and I loved that. I knew that meant something.

How different my life is now. We expect our kids to grow up, find themselves, and chart their career paths. We are suppose to have it all figured out before then. As I look back, I barely recognize the person I had been. In today's vernacular, I was a hot mess.

When Brady left home for college in the fall of 2012, I had known my biological family for 16 years. The story of finding my biological family is the story I love sharing the most. It's one of the greatest stories of reconciliation I've ever heard. It's so unbelievable. It's worthy of a Hallmark movie. I am so blessed.

So much can happen in 16 years. It should. And it did. Every time my biological family got together I walked away with more family history, family photos and great stories. I have photos of my mom, my dad, my grandparents, and my siblings as children. Photos capture family dynamics when there are no words. Oh for the love of black and white photos.

Every May 11th I celebrate the anniversary of meeting my biological mom, Beverly. She changed my life in a multitude of ways. She believed in me more than anyone ever had in my entire life. She understood brokenness. She had lived it. She had a mental breakdown, did time in a mental institution, and somehow managed to get her life together. She was my hero, for so many reasons.

When Beverly found out she was pregnant with us in 1958, her father (my grandfather) insisted that she take pills to ensure she would abort the baby. She didn't know she'd be having twins. She said she started to spot and quit taking them. For the first time in her life, she lied to her father and told him they didn't work. I remember exactly where I was when she said those words to me. She said it so casually, so matter of fact. She'd had a lifetime to get used to those words. I was stunned. "Whaaattt?!? What did you just say?" I just stood and looked at her in that moment. No words. Not a single word, just a slight tilt of my head. This was the degree of honesty and openness we shared from the beginning. The conversations we had together were refreshing and bold. I never had genuine conversations like that with my adoptive family.

When I asked her if I could use her real name when writing about our story, she said, "Sure, you can use my name in the book. Now is not the time to be coy. May all of our experiences be a blessing to whomever the Lord shall choose. I love you." And that was the way she lived life.

Beverly had lots of wisdom from a lifetime of experiences. Nothing seemed to rattle her. She took everything in stride. And, honestly I don't think much surprised her. She wasn't judgmental. She loved everyone and made room in her life for them. She confirmed my concerns about what was happening at home. There was no pulling the wool over her eyes. She always spoke the truth, but in love. She was small in stature, but lived large in so many other ways, especially her faith.

I still have one of her voice messages on my phone. Somehow it missed being deleted. On April 15, 2013 at 5:07 p.m. "Kay, this is Beverly. I was just watching the

5 o'clock news and wanted to check to be sure that you weren't in Boston at the marathon. I hadn't heard anything about you being there, so if you're at home or wherever, let me know where you are, and that you're safe. Talk to you later. Love ya." For the first time in my life someone wanted to know that I was safe. And this was how life was suppose to be. God was healing my broken heart.

Fight for Your Story

No Matter What

Sometimes in life, there is a specific event when you can say in that moment, "this changes everything." Sometimes in our lives it can be difficult to pinpoint the exact moment when that happens. Some changes happen gradually, and before you know it, you realize that life is definitely different.

My life changed dramatically when I found my biological family in 1996. But, in all honesty, my life needed to change. At the age of thirty-seven I was on my fourth marriage. Life had not been easy. I couldn't even tell you how I had gotten to that place, but it had been a lot of work. Living through my twenties was more work than it ever should have been. I hated how my life was going.

I desperately wanted a do over, but no one gets a do over in life. You just pick up the pieces and move on.

I hit a low point when marriage number four was in trouble. And then it got worse instead of better. More than anything I wanted a happy marriage. I remember hearing Jimmy Evans say in his marriage teachings that we marry according to our emotional health. I had never heard information like that before, but there was something about that statement that I could not get out of my head. First of all I had to figure out what 'emotional health' was. My childhood had left me with a deficit socially and emotionally. There was no denying I had issues.

The truth is I had been running hard and fast to escape the pain of my childhood. Children were to be seen and seldom heard. Aside from my twin sister, I was surrounded by silence, unhappiness, and anger. I didn't know that hitting and kicking weren't every child's experience. It happened at my house but I didn't understand that it didn't happen to everyone. I knew I would never strike my children, but that was all I knew. I also knew there had to be more, and my children would never know a childhood like mine.

My years growing up appeared normal from the outside but the feelings of emptiness were intense and powerful. Emptiness can seem like nothing to many people, but if you experience it you know it is definitely something. There was so much going on in my head. By all accounts I was an average kid on the outside, yet on the inside I definitely had struggles. It was another step in the healing process for me. It was becoming evident to me that if there were going to be changes, I'd have to make them on my own.

I had never had anyone to take me from crayons to perfume, that time when we learn how to deal with and identify our feelings. If our parents didn't allow us to feel emotions, or did not model healthy emotions for us, then we have a deficit in that area. I never realized that it was possible to be emotionally abandoned and still have my physical needs met.

Many of us were born into broken emotions. So, as my children grew up, I also grew. I studied successful parenting, discipline, and learning styles. Although not perfect, the childhood with my children was filled with laughter and love. I never let a day pass without telling my children how much they were loved. I often ponder those days in my heart. There was a joy I had never known before. Simply put, we had fun, day in and day out. We not only celebrated every holiday, we found a reason to celebrate every day. Each day with my children was a gift. I never took them for granted.

I hadn't anticipated the whirlwind of emotions that would follow finding my biological family. It was all part of the process, but I didn't know what I didn't know. Although I began way behind the starting line, I made great gains in a short amount of time. Life began to make more sense. I learned, I read, I listened, I observed, I studied, I grew. I became a different woman.

My journey towards emotional health continued. I studied books, listened to CDs, watched DVDs. I joined women's groups, and Bible studies, volunteered for women's conferences, followed in the footsteps of the apostle Paul to Greece and Turkey (twice), and fell more in love with Jesus.

I went through intense counseling, marriage counseling, an anger dump, and spent hours on the couches of different therapists and friends. Every step I took brought me varying degrees of freedom. I learned so I could teach my kids how to get emotionally healthy. There was no way I was wishing my life on anyone. It was like I always told my kids through the years, "Leave it the same or better than you found it." I was going to leave them better off than someone had left me.

 I've learned about myself in the most unconventional ways. God has given me revelation. It's starting to make sense. I am realizing that I don't like being alone, not because I'm an introvert, or walk in fear, but because my childhood was shrouded in silence. Those were some of the loneliest times of my life. That makes so much sense to me now.

 I was in my 50's when I took another look back, all the way back to the beginning. I revisited my journey through life. God reminded me of specific conversations, situations, and experiences. Looking back is the hardest, bravest, and most productive choice you will ever make. It's like finally letting go of every secret you were forced to keep, every little white lie you shared, and every decision you made in fear because someone threatened to abandon you if you made the wrong decision. I was uprooting years of brokenness.

Dr. Mark Rutland says: "Brokenness is the doorway through which we pass from superficiality to depth and maturity. The more often you hear someone say, this isn't really that important, you can know they have experienced brokenness at some level. The unbroken freak out over steaks not cooked properly and broken airplanes. Those who have trod through the harsh desert of brokenness know this, whatever this is, is simply not that important. Brokenness is not the end of the journey toward wholeness, it is the beginning."

Broken emotions exist when there are wounds and lies. It's simple, yet profound. Until we deal with the root, we will never get a different result. Once the root is revealed, and the wound or lie is identified, then God can fill that place with something healthy. It's as simple as bringing the light into the darkest places of our lives.

For the first time in my life I realized it wasn't all my fault. I had been impacted by my adverse childhood experiences. It had affected my childhood emotional development. The fallout from that was not subtle, and it resonated in my life for many years. No one starts out in life planning to be married four times by the age of 31. All of the would haves, could haves, and should haves wouldn't change a thing. I didn't know what I didn't know. It has taken me years to find my way in this world.

Fight for Your Story

Necessary Endings

Unfinished business will go everywhere you go. It will follow you around until it is dealt with. There was so much I still didn't understand about myself, but I was learning that feelings are the most personal part of who we are. They are important.

I remember one time in particular. I was frustrated with Blake, my oldest son. He wasn't even in school full time, but he was a pleaser and a helper. He would always make the right choice. He was such an obedient child. At one point I had him pinned to the wall and it was like I blinked I saw myself holding him against the wall. I released him and I said, "I'm so sorry. This is not about you. This is about me. Please forgive me." In that moment I realized that there was anger that needed to be dealt with. He instantly forgave me and our relationship grew. He saw me, brokenness and all. He was a giver of grace. I learned so much from my kids. I didn't know it at the time but I was teaching him to trust his feelings, and that would prove to be invaluable in his life.

    I attended an Advanced Deliverance conference in Chicago. Just driving alone to Chicago was outside my comfort zone. There were international speakers that I knew nothing about. The workshops were on healing, deliverance, prayer and more. I was intrigued and terrified at the same time. For the first time in my life I had fasted for 12 days and had been praying for a breakthrough in my marriage. I didn't know what to expect but I was driven by a desire for a freedom that so far had remained elusive. This Methodist girl was about to get way out of her comfort zone. I sat towards the back and my plan was to take notes. I was the casual observer. This skeptic had her doubts and was firmly on the fence.

    One of the presenters took a break in the middle of

his presentation and asked everyone to stand. I got really uncomfortable. I don't like it when people stray from the agenda. When he said that he wanted to pray for everyone I was relieved. Who couldn't use some prayer!?! And then he said, "Everyone raise your hands to receive what God has for you." My thought was that God could just as easily get it into my hands if my hands were in my pocket. I had never, ever lifted my hands over my head before in a church. I looked around and EVERYONE had their hands in the air. Convincing myself that I didn't know a soul there I slid my hands up to my shoulders, with my elbows tucked in nice and close. I felt like an idiot and contemplated the door in the back. I was so uncomfortable. If one person had tapped me on the shoulder and said, "This is weird, let's get out of here." I would have beat them to the door.

    Everyone now had their eyes closed as he prayed and so I closed my eyes because that is what I had been taught as a child. As he prayed I saw a black and white movie play in my head. It was all white with a silhouette walking down a street all hunched over and then he slid into an open manhole cover in the ground. Just like that I could feel something change. I had no idea what that meant but when we took our break I called my twin sister and told her what had happened. She asked me "What was it?" I said, "I have no idea." I don't know why I thought she might know! She said, "Well, ask God what it was." I said, "Well, ok. I'll call you back." I had no idea how this was suppose to work. In my most simple and basic prayer I said to God, "God, what was that movie that I saw play in my head? What did that mean?" For the first time in my life I felt God speak to me and I knew, just like that, it was rejection. With an excitement I could not contain, I called my sister and practically shouted into the phone, "It was rejection." She said, "Are you sure?" I drew in a deep breath and said, "I've never been more sure of anything in my life."

    That was a pivotal moment in my life. I didn't know if everyone got just one of those moments in life or if I could hope for another down the road. I celebrated and gave thanks to God repeatedly. Rejection? Yes, rejection. Everything seemed different. My responses were different. People responded differently to me. I didn't take their responses as personally anymore. I stopped being defensive. I had more peace in my life. I was beginning to agree that life was good. No more rose colored lenses. I didn't ever want to lose this feeling.

I had another God moment a few years later. Our marriage continued to limp along despite my breakthroughs here and there. We eventually separated but continued working on the marriage. I never gave up hope. My husband and I had gone to a marital intensive in Branson, Missouri. There was a lot of paperwork involved, assessing our needs, our strengths, our emotions, our marriage dance. I still struggled often trying to put my finger on how I was feeling. This was nothing new for me. As long as I could remember, I had a hard time identifying emotions, but when someone said it, I could say, "Yes, that's it. Exactly."

It was a beautiful program. I never felt like I was being thrown under the bus, or doing the throwing. We did the individual session, and then the couples' session. I was desperately wanting another breakthrough, but it would come in a completely different way. When the counselor said to me, "Sooo, you don't feel heard?" I thought, "this man 'gets' me. How did he do that!?!" That was what it was like my whole life growing up. Never feeling heard, and now the same thing. It was a trigger for me. It caused me to shut down. Now we were rolling. I learned so much about myself over the next 48 hours. It was all about relationships and it would prove valuable for every relationship I had or desired. It was expensive, but worth every penny. Another chunk of freedom.

 I fought hard for my marriage. I had become a different person over the years. People give up for different reasons. I'd invested a lot of time and effort. I didn't want to give up. I wanted to be a member of a team that shared my goals, dreams and vision. I wanted to be part of a family. I had never really known the unconditional love of a family.

 When the word of our separation got out I was asked by the pastoral staff to no longer teach fitness classes at the church. Yes, that was difficult, unbelievable really. But when the pastor stood in front of my participants and told them of my moral failures, multiple marriages, and disappointments, I wanted to die for the first time in a long time. I walked away from the church. I wondered how long and how often I would have to pay for my mistakes. I was feeling like the proverbial woman at the well.

After four years of being separated, the divorce papers were filed and it was time to face the death of a dream. I think one of the toughest jobs in the world is being a single parent. But, like any kind of challenge, it brings out character in you that you never knew existed. There was daily life, schedules, family life, sporting events, car shopping and selections, college visits, laundry, homework, exercise, grocery shopping, home repairs, car maintenance and so much more. Relationships go deeper, and memories are made in the good, the bad, and the beautiful times.

It's interesting when I reflect back over the years. We had so much fun, and yet some very hard times. It was in the hard times that we grew close, really close. Mothers Day weekend became a work weekend of sorts. We cleaned gutters, set out patio furniture, put out the garden hoses, swept out the fireplace, and cleaned out the basement. We changed spark plugs and tuned up the lawn mower. We cleaned out the shed, and managed to fill it up again with DIY 'projects'. We painted walls and ceilings, and ripped out old flooring. There were times when we were in way over our head, but we figured it out together.

In our spare time we watched movies. We've always been a movie watching family. They were the best of times. It's not surprising to find a line from a movie in our weekly texts. Sometimes it feels like we speak a different language. We love to get together, and to laugh together. But we've also been through some tough stuff together.

I learned how to respond when my child had been arrested or was about to fail or quit school. I had to figure it out without losing the relationship. Nothing is worth that. I had to figure out when to let go, and when to hold on tighter. I learned about drug rehab and what my options were. Sometimes I had to push back when they said there were no options. I didn't settle for the status quo. I had to make the hard calls and the difficult decisions. But in the end, I fought for my children in ways that no one had ever fought for me.

Necessary Beginnings

Of this one thing I am sure, I am a lifelong learner. Despite being a learner, it was still difficult for me to take steps towards healing. Academic learning is much easier than emotional growth. I wanted to run away from home more as an adult than I ever wanted to as a child. And, trust me, that was a lot. Dealing with pain is not for the faint of heart. It takes determination, willpower, faith, and one heck of a support team.

At times like that it's easy, and tempting, to shrink back in life. Live small. Stay safe. I recognize when I've been hurt by life because that old familiar rejection wants to creep in, and my coping mechanism is to disconnect.

It's easy. It's safe. My comfort zone got small, but ironically it didn't bring me what it promised. . . comfort. I have learned when you find comfort in your comfort zone, it's time to move on. Outside your comfort zone you will find new challenges, growth, resources, relationships, and opportunities. Naturally there will be adjustments you will need to make along the way, and you will always wish it had been easier.

There was no doubt that God was restoring the years that the locust had eaten. It didn't happen overnight and it wasn't easy. There were years of unhealthy ways of thinking, and broken emotions that needed to be dealt with. What does that even look like? How does one 'find oneself' at the age of fifty something?

There were buckets of tears, hours of soul searching, and lots of observing. And in it all, I found people who were trustworthy and people who were not. I found out what it means to be a friend, and to have a friend. I found out it was ok to say no even when it was unpopular, but necessary. I drew on the strengths I had developed as a child. I was a survivor. I had to be a survivor to get through my childhood. Plain and simple. I had grit and a high ACE score.

I confided in a counselor and it felt good to verbalize what had been sworn to secrecy for so many years. A big chunk of healing came when he said, "You have had no one you could trust your entire life. No one has been there for you." I knew it was true. And he knew it was true, and that was enough for me. He was helping me make sense of this broken life of mine.

David Augsburger says, "Being heard is so close to being loved that for the average person they are almost indistinguishable." I can't think of a statement that is more profound when it comes to being heard. It was especially true in my life.

The term emotional intelligence refers to your ability to recognize and understand emotions in yourself and others, and then your ability to use this new self-awareness to manage your behavior and your relationships. This allows you to connect with people and to feel what others feel. Strong emotional intelligence is a trademark characteristic of effective leaders and healthy people.

When it comes to expressing and processing emotions, people either internalize their problems or externalize them. Internalizers believe it's up to them to make the necessary changes. Externalizers are more likely to look for someone to do it for them. I knew immediately I was an internalizer. I'm a stuffer too. I probably have a tendency to over think, and over process. Ok. Not probably, but definitely. To my defense, that's all I knew from growing up. It was my personality. I've always been contemplative.

I'd spent my childhood observing everything around me. I studied people and situations. I was a curious child, and I didn't miss much. The problem was that I didn't know what to do with all those observations, but one day I would.

Some say that emotions can't be trusted, but I believe if we use our emotions as information, they will guide us to a healthier place. We have to be willing to want more, to reach for more, to take a leap of faith.

Emotions play a role in our healing process. If we allow ourselves to experience and explore each emotion we are able to go from unhealthy emotions to healthy emotions. Choosing to do nothing is seldom the best option. Exploring emotions includes taking risks, feeling vulnerable, and ultimately loving ourselves. It is the bravest and most rewarding thing you will ever do for yourself.

For me, the handwriting was on the wall. It was alcohol or a marathon. For me it was one foot in front of the other. I was running early mornings or late evenings. No one around me really knew why. They thought it was the athlete in me, when in all actuality it was the lesser of two evils. I recorded some major miles every month. When I started I was running on empty. I kept looking outside myself because the pain to look inside was just too great. My saving grace became the teachings, the TED Talks, and the music I would listen to while running. And then before I knew it I found myself just running for the love of running. Every step brought me some degree of freedom. I was finding myself. And I was liking the person I was finding.

Emotional healing is like running a marathon. It begins with a step. And then you realize that you can actually run for one minute at a time, and then two. And when you can run a mile there will be cheering, confetti, and a lot of high fives. You will want to post on social media when you finish your first 5k, because the world looks different, but it's not the world that is changing, it's that you are changing, growing, living life. You will want to share your progress with your friends because there will be a part of you that wants everyone to experience what you are experiencing. The longer distances you run, the more training is required. You will be running for a couple of hours to complete your first half marathon (13.1 miles), but when they slip that medal around your neck you mentally make the decision to run a full marathon (26.2 miles). You kind of panic when you wonder how you got to this place. But let's be honest, you haven't felt this good in years. Every step brings you a certain degree of freedom and you love who you are becoming.

That's running, and emotional healing. It's a choice, and it's scary and overwhelming at times. There will be moments when you want to throw in the towel. Everyone has moments like that, and there may be days when you have several in a row. You have to remember how normal that is. Training prepares you for the marathons in life, but with hope as our cheerleader, the impossible becomes possible.

One of my greatest lessons I've learned in life is how men and women are different, and yet the same. A woman's greatest need is to feel safe. When a woman feels safe, she allows access to her heart by being vulnerable. This is where life is rich, intimacy is amazing, and deep relationship happens. When a woman doesn't feel safe physically, spiritually, or emotionally she will build a wall around her heart. Think of her heart as the holy of holies. Not everyone has access to this part of her life. This is the place where, as women, we decide who gets in and who doesn't. When we feel safe our defenses drop and intimacy happens.

A man's greatest need is respect. A man who is respected will respond with open access to his heart. However, if a man doesn't feel respected, he quickly closes access to his heart and intimacy suffers. When this happens, people are responding more out of fear, and less out of love. What really needs to happen is for us to look at the heart and intentions of the other person. When we look at their heart, rather than their words, we can offer grace in moments of epic failure. Remember, you most likely married according to your emotional health, so learning new ways of communicating and seeing each other will also increase your emotional intelligence. It won't come naturally at first, but before long it will feel very natural. You will need to lean in when everything in you wants to turn and run.

I've also learned that the foundation for well-adjusted kids starts with parents. So, if you are a parent or in a parental role, the most important job you have is to give your children what they need to be successful adults. Their future literally rests in your hands. Successful parenting isn't passive, and it isn't easy. If it didn't happen in your childhood, the journey is different, and sometimes difficult, but definitely possible.

I feel like success starts with realizing what is possible. If you don't dare to dream, you are limiting not only yourself, but the contribution you were intended to make in this world. Everyone should leave a positive footprint in this world.

Necessary Pain

Suffering in life produces endurance, and then endurance produces character, and finally character produces hope. Hope is our anchor and our buoy. It keeps us afloat when life is so incredibly hard. We have to choose hope in those moments. It is only through suffering, endurance, and character development that we get to hope.

Job 11:18

Then you would trust, because there is hope;
And you would look around and rest securely.

> Faith goes up the stairs that love has built
> and looks out the window which hope has opened.
> ~ Charles Spurgeon

> Hardship often prepares an ordinary person
> for an extraordinary destiny.
> ~ C.S. Lewis

I don't think anyone would every choose hardship, trials, pain, rejection, loss, disappointment, and heartbreak. I've observed situations in life where I wonder how people survive horrific circumstances, tremendous loss, and outright betrayal. In all honesty I shake my head and give thanks that it didn't happen to me. Most times I don't think I'm tough enough to weather those kinds of storms. My heart breaks for childhood illness, the loss of life at a young age, and circumstances that take the breath from your lungs and leave you in a heap on the floor. And yet, we all go through pain on different levels. Pain in life is utterly unavoidable.

Pain will take you on a journey you did not and would not sign up for. In a way, trying to avoid pain in life will, in and of itself, be painful. There is no escaping it. Pain can be purifying and bring about re-evaluation and renewed vision. While we would not sign up for painful trials, we would not survive without them. They are what produces character in our lives.

For as long as I could remember I was more of a daddy's girl. How fortunate for me to have had two fathers. My biological father, Calvin, died in 1998, just 22 months after I met him. I was grateful for the time we had together, but in all honestly I had always hoped it would had been longer. He changed my life. Even though he didn't exactly have his life together, he breathed life into me. And after a lifetime of wondering who I looked like, I finally knew I was the spitting image of my biological father.

My adoptive dad will always be 'dad' to me. He taught me how to ride a bike and tinker in the garage. He taught me how to mow the lawn with a mower that had a rotary blade and no motor. We spent time golfing and working on projects together. He loved to take care of his flower garden and tend to his yard.

He also taught me what an angry man looks like. If

you lived outside of our home, chances are slim you ever experienced or witnessed his wrath. There were times when he would kick the dog or throw walnuts at the dog when he got angry. Those times sent me running to rescue the dog. I don't think the neighbors ever put two and two together. I knew when he had that angry roll of the tongue there was going to be hell to pay, but in all honesty, the fear and anticipation that went with it were just as painful.

My dad was into finance and he was pretty good at it. Finance was not something that came easy for me, but there are lessons you just pick up after living with an accountant. I remember as a little girl how my dad helped us put the coins in the pages of our coin collections. One for me, and one for my sister. I remember stacks and stacks of blue folders of old coin sets, the shiny new coins, and the hope chest and cedar closet which were their secret hiding place. We not only built a coin collection together, but there were so many memories tucked into those old blue pages. My dad always celebrated when the special mint coins arrived in the mail. He said he was going to have a million dollars when he retired, and I believed him.

While my adoptive dad was not exactly the picture of health, he did quit smoking when they adopted us. I will always be grateful for that expression of love. After he had open heart surgery, a few strokes, and overall declining health, my dad made me the executor of my parents' will. He showed me what to do in the event of their death. They had made all of their own funeral arrangements with the funeral home and church. He especially wanted me to have the hope chest and my coin collection.

After another tumble and a broken hip, he landed himself in the care center where they could watch him and help him mend. The health issues were more often and more serious. The staff said he would never leave. One day he told me what they had said. I'd never seen my dad so hopeless. His lip quivered, and for the first time I saw a tear. I held his hand and I promised him we would work hard together to see if he could get strong enough to go home. We lifted weights and exercised three times a week from his wheelchair. Some days he only took 2 steps on his own, but it was progress. I know the nurses thought we were nuts, but I noticed the way they looked at us as he got stronger. We made that hallway ring with laughter as we reminisced about the stories of my youth. We were a team and I was so proud to be his daughter. I never left without telling him I loved him, and he told me he loved me too.

He finally passed the test to go back home to the retirement community on July 13, 2011, and he never stopped smiling once he got there. We still exercised and he shared his favorite stories about every resident as we walked the carpeted hallways. I was so proud of him! I treasure those memories.

My mother hated having him home. It meant more work for her. She was mad at me for helping him come home. She never had anything nice to say to me after that. And, truthfully, she seldom spoke to me, but always to my sister. My sister often said, "I don't know why she's always so rude to you." I shrugged my shoulders, but on the inside, it broke my heart. After just eight short weeks, my dad was suddenly gone to be with Jesus.

In hindsight there were clues through the years, but I couldn't bring myself to believe that my own mom didn't like me or that she would ever betray me. Because after all, we were family, and well, family is family. However, I finally realized that appearances were important to her, and for her to have a successful son-in-law was far more coveted than having a daughter whom she perceived as a dud. It didn't matter how many changes I made in my life, it would have never been enough.

I do have some wonderful memories of my mom when I was a little girl. I'll always remember when my mom picked me up from school when I was in the first grade and I was standing outside the office with diarrhea running down my legs and tears running down my face. She rescued me and took me home. She cried with me when I wet the bed at night and didn't mean to. I just couldn't help it. I tried so hard. I remember how she helped with Brownies, Daisies, and Girl Scouts. And I remember when my book cover matched my dress in elementary school, because my mom had made both.

There were also times of great sadness. Growing up in our home was very quiet, except for the outbursts of anger that sent us scampering for cover until the dust settled. We never really knew what the triggers were, hard as we tried to figure it out. I remember as a little girl standing on my tippy toes so I could look in the bathroom mirror and saying, "Please God, make me pretty so someone will listen to me." It was a prayer of absolute desperation, to a God I didn't even know existed.

    My adoptive mom had told me that one time her mother (my grandma) told her "that she had made her bed, and now she had to sleep in it". I'm positive she didn't like that answer because she never forgot it. But when she passed that advice on to me, there was no way I was settling for what she had. Ironically she had moments of good advice, moments of bad advice, and it was just enough to keep me confused for most of my life. As a child and a fairly mixed up adult, I didn't recognize that her unhappiness was connected to when she was around my dad. She was always trying to fill that void, and it often came through the relationships I had, and what she could gain from them.

    The hardest thing I ever had to do was tell my parents that I was pregnant my junior year in high school, and my mom said I needed to control my emotions. I had no idea how to do that, or even what that meant. I don't really think she knew either. The disappointments that followed were bigger, and more high profile. Divorces always make the paper. She became bitter and angry. She never acknowledged that I had gotten my life together, but I had.

Holding onto resentment will always comes at a price. My mom didn't want anyone to know she was losing her mind. Her behavior was textbook dementia. Her brain scans revealed what she was trying to hide. I remember one time when we had a care meeting for my dad and she left the car running out front the whole time. She couldn't find her keys, and when we found her car running, we found her keys. There were other clues. It was a steady and rapid decline. In just thirteen short months, she was also gone.

The remaining boxes from my parent's house surrounded me. I stood alone, and in utter silence. The documents from the attorney were still in my hand. I hadn't seen this coming. I'd spent the last 20 years of my life making good decisions, and honoring my parents. I had been singled out, cut from my parents' inheritance, and rejected again. I was no longer the executor of the will. Ironically, the hope chest was mine, but my cherished coin collection was long gone. No explanations, no earthly inheritance.

The people my mom thought she could trust betrayed her wishes. They encouraged her to change her will. They took her money, her treasures, my coin collection and wrote me out of her will. Her attorney should have contacted the family, but she did not. Towards the end of my mom's life, my mom told my aunt that she was afraid she had made a mistake, but didn't know how to fix it. My inheritance was split between my sister, my children, my former step-children, and my former spouse. Now there was nothing left but a faltering pinky promise between sisters and more questions than answers.
It's just as hard to be a child and think you are unwanted as it is to be an adult and have it confirmed. I'm not going to lie, there were tough days ahead filled with overwhelming sadness and confusion as I worked through the madness and chaos.

Sometimes life simply cannot be put into words. It was one of those times for me when I just shook my head, because there were no words. My journal sat blank for a long time. Not a single word. I wanted to curl up and die really. I cried about it. I wished it would go away. I asked myself over and over, "Why did this happen to me?" I revisited my counselor, my therapist, my friend. It's important to have a safe place where we can throw it all on the table and say "This isn't right." And he said to me, "You're right." And the healing began. It was quite a process. No anger, no bitterness, no voodoo dolls. Trust me, I was tempted again and again, but I chose the high road. I chose to forgive them all. Not for their benefit, but for my benefit. I made peace with what was behind me.

You know when your broken heart breaks someone else's heart, you have found someone worthy of your trust. Beverly became that person to me. She was my mom once again. What a beautiful journey we shared. She said what I should have heard growing up. She initiated the healing process in me the day she said, "I've waited my whole life for you to come back to me."

On February 15, 2016, Beverly breathed her last breath. She sat down to rest, and never woke up. We had shared nearly twenty years together. I had so many beautiful memories to reflect on, and not a single regret. Over the years we had shared so many conversations, memories, photographs, letters, emails and voice messages. Every memory made me smile.

Making the decision to find my biological family was one of the bravest and best decisions I have ever made in my life. The search and the end result were life changing. I never could have anticipated the healing that would happen from that 21 day adventure back in 1996. Finding my parents and being welcomed back into my biological family is not the typical result, but it was our experience. I'm fortunate to have a relationship with all of my siblings. Honestly, I never saw that coming.

I realize that life is a journey. I wouldn't trade a moment of this journey. I'm not saying I would have chosen it if I had the opportunity. These experiences have made me who I am today. There have been many, many days when I wanted to quit. There have also been several times in my life when I thought I would not make it. I don't understand the reason, but I thank God for the result.

For most of my life I believed that I had wonderful parents and that I was the problem. I don't know why it was so hard for me to admit that they didn't know how to love me, or each other. That was the saddest truth I ever had to accept. They controlled me and criticized me. They knew how to make me feel guilty and manipulate me. I

grew up confused about what love really was and what it looked like. I searched far and wide for feelings of acceptance, safety, value and respect. All I ever wanted was to love, to be loved, and to be heard.
.

Fight for Your Story

Good, Better, Best

Life can be seen though the lens of what is good, what is better, and what is best. From the beverages we drink, to the food we eat, and to the way we live life, we can always find ways to go from 'good' to 'best'. Getting from the good to the best places in life doesn't happen by accident. Change worth pursuing happens intentionally. Living at an intentional level is the place where growth and comfort cannot coexist.

As an adult I am making sense of my life. I now am able to see what other people don't see because of where I've been in life. I am a loss expert. I have known loss in ways that many of my friends have never known.

However, at the same time, I now know more fullness of joy and laughter than at any other time in my life.

It's like standing at the top of the Hancock Building in Chicago after hustling up 94 floors, and looking out over the city. With my heart beating wildly and my lungs on fire, I see more than someone who rode the elevator to the top. They won't appreciate it like I do. It cost me more. My investment was greater. The colors seem richer, and the scenery can't be described. The 1,632 steps changed me. I wasn't the same person that had started the climb 18 minutes earlier. It wasn't just the people around me and the challenge to finish. It was the experience. It's about who I became in the process.

It's also like running a half marathon with your college age boys. That half marathon changed all of our lives and it changed our relationship. It's really not even all about how far we went. You really get to know someone when you run 13.1 miles with them. Destination runs around the country have become an annual event for us now, and that selfie at mile marker 8 has become a tradition. That picture speaks volumes. It serves as a reminder of where we've been, and how far we've come.

Hungering for more in life will take you where mere curiosity will never get you. For my entire life I knew there had to be more. I was never content to just settle.

I see people differently. I have bold conversations. I appreciate people, their experiences and the lessons they've learned in life. I want to learn from them. I don't have time to make all of the mistakes in life. Heaven knows I've made my share.

Interestingly enough these experiences are making every picture in my life more colorful. The backgrounds in my photos no longer seem empty. Every day is like that for me.

I can stand in an elementary classroom and see wonder, sadness, and joy in children. I see how their personality starts to come out when they begin to relax and trust you. I see how far a kind word can go in the broken down life of a child. Every student has a story to tell, and if we are able to look beyond the dysfunctional behavior, there is a strength behind it. My heart aches for them, but I see their potential. Let's tell kids what's right about them.

Once upon a time I was in a similar place. My experiences help me to see the whole picture.

The Center for Disease Control says my adverse childhood experiences should make me an adult with adverse health outcomes. My experiences put me in the traumatic category. I should be an obese, chain smoking, alcoholic, who is battling IV and illicit drug use, with sexually transmitted diseases, and who has attempted suicide. There is no doubt I am a loss expert. And yet God has redeemed my life. I have none of those issues. Through it all, God taught me about the love of a Father, and the goodness of God. When I asked God how he could use this mess I made, he showed me. I have a heart to help the hurting, the helpless and the hopeless because, well, that's who I used to be. God has been so very good to me.

I don't know why God entrusted this life to me. I don't understand why He felt the need to give me more than my share. It feels like more than my share. Maybe He knew I'd tell the world. Maybe He knew this tender little heart wouldn't quit until I found a little bit of love. I'm sure He knew I'd never be happy until I shared my journey to help others. We need to find the courage, resiliency, strength, grace and love to positively impact those around us. In the words of Mother Teresa, "Never worry about numbers. Help one person at a time and always start with the person nearest you."

I'll never know what it means to have the unconditional love of parents who are suppose to love you and tell you that you always have a place to come home to. I'll never know that safety and security. I may never know what it's like to have financial security, at least not in the traditional sense.

God has chosen to bless me in other ways. I had the overwhelming love of a birth mother for nearly 20 years. She was my cheerleader. She loved me unconditionally. She brought healing to my heart time and time again. She will always be my hero.

My biological family grew to eight brothers and four sisters. When I asked God for a brother as I was growing up, I had no idea that He actually heard my prayers and was blessing me beyond belief. Family has been, and will always be everything to me.

My children are a blessing to me. I chose to interrupt the cycle of childhood emotional neglect. God blessed my efforts as a parent, and filled in the gaps. My children have more emotional intelligence in their 20's and 30's than I did in my 40's. We learn from each other. I have given them all I have to give. There are no secrets. My life is an open book to them. I don't have all of the answers in life, but they know I will always be there for them.

I am blessed when I hear of successful adoption stories. Mine was not one to start with, but it is now. I am always impressed by birth moms who have chosen to give their children up for adoption. They are the real heroes. I know the heartache of abortion, the feeling of being out of options, and choosing the lesser of two evils. Fear always drives that decision. I wish we were a community of people who would help to make others journeys easier. I wish there were more open doors, more open arms, and less criticism and judgment. So many stories would be different.

I was determined that the wounds that I had experienced during my lifetime would have a purpose. When I would meet people and listen to their stories I would say time and time again, "I understand." And, I really did.

Our lives are a collection of stories. They are the truth about who we are, what we believe, where we came from, how we struggle, and yet they also proclaim how we are strong. We need to let go of what people think, and celebrate our story. This is not the story I would have ever written for myself. You will either accept your story and own it, or you will end up being defined by your story. Find your passion, and fight for your story.

Fight for Your Story

An excerpt from the companion workbook
<u>Fighting for Your Story</u>

As I shared stories and situations, and decisions that I made, I hope that you have been challenged and encouraged to explore your own story. My goal is to help you, the reader, make a similar journey from brokenness to restoration, from loneliness to community, and from despair to hope. My driving force in writing this book was to share the journey that I took so that others would consider making their journey towards freedom. I hope we can share in this journey together.

Everyone has a story worth telling. Sometimes the details are just under the surface, sometimes there is some pain to work through, and there are even times where it is downright hard getting to the truth. Our goal is to become healthier, and happier. I believe with my whole heart that our best days are ahead.

Fighting for your story is not easy. It will probably be one of the hardest journeys you will ever make. But it will also pay you the biggest dividends. Every relationship that you have will be enriched, honest, and more fulfilling. Most of all, your relationships will go deeper, get richer, and transform your life. You have nothing to lose, and everything to gain. Many times what we won't do for ourselves, we will do for the benefit of our children. Maybe it will be your children and grandchildren who will reap the benefits of healthy emotions.

The pages that follow are meant to be thought provoking and contemplative. They are intended to be worked on slowly and as you feel led. Don't rush through. There is no timeline. To do it right you will need to meditate and reflect on your life experiences, and in some cases come to terms with the wrongs you have committed, and those committed against you. It may drive you to the couch of a therapist or the shoulder of a dear friend. Don't hesitate to reach out to those who are skilled in these areas. This is not the time to shrink back. Reach out and look to what is possible. Greater days are ahead.

John 8:31-32

If you abide in My word,
then you are truly disciples of Mine;
And you shall know the truth,
and the truth shall make you free.

The Greek word for knowledge is *ginosko*. It tells us there is something that must be known, something that must be recognized, and something that must be acknowledged. And THAT truth will set us free.

Knowing something is just information and only the first step. It's what to do with that knowledge that has the potential to change your life. In the knowing there is also something that must be recognized. There is a key to your freedom in recognition. Sometimes we have a fresh revelation, like connecting the dots. It's like seeing it differently for the first time. It will look and feel different.

And finally, it's the acknowledging. That may mean that you acknowledge your role in it, or how it impacted you. It may mean acknowledging that what you have chosen to believe is a lie, and the truth is downright painful. That may require you to let that wall down that's around your heart. It's there for a reason, so respect it and try to begin to dismantle it. Those areas in our lives where we redeem the pain become powerful areas in our lives. We all experience pain in life, but if our pain isn't resolved it will limit us. We will only grow to the level of our emotional pain.

Some of us have memories buried so deep they are not coming out in this lifetime, not as long as we are in charge. We have every intention of taking them to the grave with us. The problem with that thinking is that we may make it to the grave sooner because of our unexpressed emotions. Emotions that are suppressed, hidden, and denied have power. They are changing you on the inside, and the outside. They manifest themselves whether you validate them or not. They don't need your approval or acknowledgement. If you don't deal with the underlying issue, it doesn't go away on its own.

Years of research show that these 'things' are having an adverse affect on our health, and quality of life. Not to mention the impact it has had on our children. Adverse childhood experiences left unaddressed become adverse adult health outcomes. Wisdom empowers us to choose a lifestyle that brings health, strength and long life, rather than sickness, weakness and shortness of days.

We need to deal with what is keeping us stuck. Even a step in the right direction will bear fruit in your life. We need to heal our hearts. Some of us are holding onto wounds because we don't know what else to do with them. I hope you will join me as together we process them, learn from them, and send them on their way. But we aren't stopping there. We need to replace them with something healthy so that our final condition is better. We will replace anger with forgiveness. We will replace shame with vulnerability. We will replace fear with love. This is a process, and it works. In writing our story we will forgive, repair, repent, love and bless. Every story will have a happy ending.

For as long as I can remember I struggled to identify emotions. I simply couldn't put my feelings into words. I didn't know what I didn't know, but I did know that I didn't know enough. I would have scored zero on self awareness. So, we are celebrating your starting point, because that first step is often times the hardest.

As we contemplate our own stories, it helps to have boundaries to keep us safe. Let's think of these as suggestions to keep us safe through the writing process.

- Feel the pain.
- Embrace the message in the pain.
- Know when to move on. Don't dwell there.

There are no rules as to the lengthy of your story. It can be short and to the point. It can be typed or on a notecard. Maybe yours will look like a bullet list. It can include every shocking detail, or maybe you're not quite there yet. It's a process. Sometimes the writing process stirs something within and the words just flow. Some days you will experience writers block. Every chapter and story will be unique. The writing process can be agonizing, painful, healing, liberating. Your heart may race. There may be layers upon layers to work through. The end result will be worth every emotion you encounter along the way.

In order to get healthy, you have to identify what is keeping you up at night.

Most likely these will be your best kept secrets. They are the ones you haven't spoken out loud, and I'm guessing you probably haven't even written them down. We keep our own secrets far better than we keep the secrets of others. We're going after the tough stuff, the stuff others have given up on. The stuff nobody knows about. The stuff you're too ashamed to share. Yes, **that** stuff.

Let's begin by looking at a few key emotions, and what we can learn when we explore each emotion and the effect it has had on us.

bit·ter·ness

/bid-ər-nəs/

noun

> unresolved anger and disappointment at being treated unfairly; resentment

---

Bitterness is a choice, and left unresolved it will consume you. It is anger taken to the next level and it will affect you, and everyone around you. In fact, it will cause others to stop wanting to be around you. Bitterness will not only harden your heart on the inside, it has a way of hardening your look on the outside. We become bitter when we believe that the other person will not be punished like we would punish them. It is easy to become bitter and it can happen before you realize it. It is our way of judging them in order to be treated fairly. But it doesn't work that way. Dwelling on what has happened to us is emotionally exhausting and causes the root of bitterness to go deeper.

Hebrews 12:15

See to it that no one comes short of the grace of God; that no root of bitterness springing up causes trouble, and by it many be defiled.

Ephesians 4:31-32

Get rid of all bitterness, rage, anger, harsh words, and slander, as well as all types of malicious behavior. And be kind to one another, tenderhearted, forgiving one another, even as God in Christ forgave you.

Bitterness causes you to close your heart little by little. As your heart gets hard you smile less, laugh less and love less. You live smaller because your world gets smaller. You are less kind, and more angry. You have less friends, and you care less. The only person you really care about is you. And the only person that matters to you is you. You become the topic of your conversations, and your world. And that really is a very sad reality.

Fight for Your Story

Several years ago, my sister and I went to pray for a family friend. She was in the beginning stages of Parkinson's Disease and we had been asked to pray for her health. As we started to pray I kept hearing the word 'unforgiveness'. I turned to my sister and said, "I keep hearing unforgiveness, are you hearing anything?" She said she was hearing the same thing. I turned to this woman and innocently asked, "Is there anyone that you need to forgive?" Well, I had stumbled on a topic not open for debate without even knowing it. She said, "My sister wronged me several years ago, and I will NEVER forgive her." Then she said it again with the emphasis on never, "I will NEVERRRRR forgive her." It didn't matter what we said, what scripture we quoted, she wasn't going to forgive and that was the end of the story. It literally was the end of her story as we watched that disease accelerate and literally take her life. She went from a soft woman to a stooped and harsh looking woman in less than a year. Not long after that she was gone. We were stunned. That day we learned the consequences of unforgiveness, and what the root of bitterness looked like.

There always needs to be a willingness to forgive on our part. We need to choose forgiveness whenever God reveals it to us. It may be that you cannot get someone off your mind. Forgive them. Pray for them. Bless them. Do those things especially when you don't feel like it. Forgiving others is not an option. It's required, and it is the number one step in removing bitterness. If you find yourself constantly saying negative things about someone, could it be that a root of bitterness is trying to grow in your heart?

Colossians 3:12-13
So, as those who have been chosen of God,
holy and beloved, put on a heart of compassion,
kindness, humility, gentleness, and patience;
bearing with one another, and forgiving each other,
whoever has a complaint against anyone;
just as the Lord forgave you, so also should you.

Here is a sample prayer of forgiveness you can pray or feel free to pray one of your own:

Lord, forgive me for my part in this. I choose to forgive (fill in the blank). I am asking you to bless them in all they do. Thank you for showing me where bitterness may have taken root in my life. Please help me to repair and restore the relationships that have been impacted by my bitterness. In Jesus' name, Amen.

When you forgive someone, remember you are also making the decision to never bring this situation up again to anyone else, not even yourself. It is finished.

Fighting Bitterness For Your Story

If you hate the way you feel when you think of (fill in the blank), you were never intended to let it take root in your life. It's not for you to judge, and it's not who you are. If thinking of them gets your buttons pushed, then that's what needs to come to an end. It's being brave enough to ask the question, "Why am I really feeling this way?" It could be something you have been dragging around since childhood. Be willing to let it go. There is amazing freedom when you are willing to 'go there'.

And when it is all said and done, we will have replaced anger with forgiveness.

Remember that there is something that must be known, something that must be recognized, and something that must be acknowledged. And THAT truth will set us free. Keep in mind that it may be finding out the truth about a situation, about another person, or about yourself that will begin the freedom process. So with that in mind, what are the events or circumstances that have caused you to become bitter?

_____

_____

_____

_____

_____

_____

_____

Fight for Your Story

And now, consider the question 'Why'? Getting to the 'why' may take more work than your 'what'.

Fight for Your Story

Change happens when we say, "No matter what, I'm going to forgive (fill in the blank)", and I am not ever going to bring it up again. What is it you're NOT going to (do, say, watch, speak, pursue, respond to) anymore?

_____

_____

_____

_____

_____

_____

_____

_____

_____

_____

No matter what, I am going to (fill in the blank). You may pray for them daily, or you may pray blessings into their life. When you choose to let them off the hook, it does allow you to let go of negative emotions like bitterness and anger, which will ultimately set you free. In the beginning you may have to do it through gritted teeth. I certainly did.

_____

_____

_____

_____

_____

_____

_____

_____

_____

_____

Fight for Your Story

To Whom It May Concern is a story of love, and sacrifice, and wholeness. Experience first-hand the letters written by a mother in 1958 and finally discovered by her twin daughters in 1996. Celebrate the discovery of three sets of twins, separated by adoption, and the blessed reunion with their family of origin. This hardcover book contains envelopes on the pages to be opened by the reader. ISBN 978-0-9701781-0-7.

Fight for Your Story

About the Author

Kay is an inspirational storyteller and motivational speaker with more life experiences than most people you know. She has demonstrated resilience, perseverance, and unbelievable strength as she has defied the odds. She relates well to people of all ages, and her story challenges people to embrace their life and make the most of it. She discusses difficult topics like adoption, abortion, divorce, family dynamics, suicide, faith, and hope in the face of adversity. Kay has a passion to see people live healthy in all areas of their life.

Kay has a B.A. in health education from The University of Northern Iowa and began pursuing a masters in 2017. She has over 25 years experience in the fitness and health industry. She lives in the Midwest and has three grown children, and five granddaughters.

There is more information on her website regarding the workbook, Fighting for Your Story, that accompanies this book.

Fight for Your Story

Contact Information:

Website: kaycervetti.org

Website: thetrainingcenterusa.org

Email: cervettikay@gmail.com

Facebook: facebook.com/kaycervetti

Twitter: Twitter.com/@kaycervetti

www.ingramcontent.com/pod-product-compliance
Lightning Source LLC
LaVergne TN
LVHW051508070426
835507LV00022B/2982